WHAT WHERE WHY ?

Do French Fries Come from France?

By Ronne Randall

Gareth Stevens Publishing
A WORLD ALMANAC EDUCATION GROUP COMPANY

Please visit our web site at: www.garethstevens.com
For a free color catalog describing Gareth Stevens Publishing's list of high-quality books and multimedia programs, call 1-800-542-2595 (USA) or 1-800-387-3178 (Canada). Gareth Stevens Publishing's fax: (414) 332-3567.

Library of Congress Cataloging-in-Publication Data

Randall, Ronne.
    Do French fries come from France? / by Ronne Randall.
       p. cm. — (What? Where? Why?)
    Includes index.
    Summary: Explains, in simple text and illustrations, the origins of a variety of foods, including bread, French fries, eggs, ketchup, and milk.
    ISBN 0-8368-3787-8 (lib. bdg.)
    1. Food industry and trade—Juvenile literature. [1. Food.
2. Food industry and trade.] I. Title. II. Series.
TP370.3.R36   2003
641—dc21
                                     2003045774

This North American edition first published in 2004 by
Gareth Stevens Publishing
A World Almanac Education Group Company
330 West Olive Street, Suite 100
Milwaukee, Wisconsin 53212 USA

Original copyright © 2003 by ticktock Entertainment Ltd. First published in Great Britain in 2003 by ticktock Media Ltd., Unit 2, Orchard Business Centre, North Farm Road, Tunbridge Wells, Kent, TN2 3XF, England. This U.S. edition copyright © 2004 by Gareth Stevens, Inc.

Gareth Stevens series editor: Dorothy L. Gibbs
Gareth Stevens cover design: Melissa Valuch

Picture Credits
[Abbreviations: (t) top, (b) bottom, (c) center, (l) left, (r) right]
Alamy Images: front cover, pages 1(tl), 4(bl), 5(tc), 8(br), 9(tl), 11(c), 12(bl, tr), 13(t), 15(tl, cr), 16(tl), 18(br), 19(t, cl), 20(bl, tl), 22(bc), 24(b).
Corbis: pages 1(bl, cl, c, tr, cr, br), 2(all), 3(all), 4(tl, tc, tr), 5(tl, tr, b), 6(tl), 7(tr, c, b), 8(tr), 10(all), 11(bl, tl, tr), 12(tl, br), 13(bl, cl), 14(all), 15(tr), 16(bl, tr), 17(all), 19(cr), 20(br), 21(br, ct), 22(bl, tl, tr), 23(tr, br), 24(tl, tr).
Science Photo Library: page 19(cr).

With thanks to: Lorna Cowan, Rod Knutton, and Elizabeth Wiggans.

Printed in Hong Kong

1 2 3 4 5 6 7 8 9 07 06 05 04 03

CONTENTS

Introduction ... 4

Do french fries come from France? ... 6

What food is made from tomatoes? ... 8

What is bread made from? ... 10

Where do eggs come from? ... 12

Which foods come from cows? ... 14

Where does orange juice come from? ... 16

What kind of a plant is rice? ... 18

What is chocolate made from? ... 20

Glossary ... 22

Index ... 24

Words in the glossary are printed in **boldface** type the first time they appear in the text.

Have you ever wondered where the food you eat comes from?

supermarket   **bakery**   **farm**

You probably buy most of your food at a supermarket.
You might also get some kinds of foods from a bakery
or a **produce** market — or even from a farm.

Have you ever wondered how food gets to a supermarket
or a bakery? Have you ever wondered how foods are
made or what they are made from?

Do french fries come from France?

French fries come from potatoes. Potatoes grow in fields on farms.

You can grow potatoes in your garden, too.

When potatoes get old, they start to **sprout**.

potato sprout

If you plant sprouting potatoes in the ground, they will grow into potato plants!

The sprouts grow into **shoots**.

The shoots grow upward through the soil and become potato plants, with flowers.

When the flowers turn yellow and die, it's time to dig the potatoes out of the soil.

What crunchy snack food is made from potatoes?

(answer on page 23)

To make french fries, the potatoes are washed, and the skins are peeled off.

Then the potatoes are cut into sticks. The sticks are deep-fried in hot oil.

Enjoy your french fries!

What food made from tomatoes tastes good with french fries?

a) mustard

b) mayonnaise

c) vinegar

d) ketchup

(Turn the page to find out.)

What food is made from tomatoes?

Ketchup is made from tomatoes. Tomatoes grow on plants.

Tomato plants grow in gardens and on farms. Before they are **ripe**, tomatoes are green.

Is a tomato a vegetable or a fruit?

(answer on page 23)

Ripe tomatoes are red. They are ready to be picked. On a farm, a machine picks them and puts them into **bins**.

Trucks take the tomatoes to a ketchup factory.

At the factory, the tomatoes are crushed in a **vat**.

The crushed tomatoes are mixed with salt, sugar, spices, and vinegar.

The mixture is cooked, cooled, and put into bottles.

vat

Do you put ketchup on hamburgers or french fries?

What is bread made from?

a) wheat

b) flowers

c) beans

d) potatoes

(Turn the page to find out.)

9

What is bread made from?

Bread is made from wheat. Farmers plant wheat in fields.

wheat ear

As a wheat plant grows, an **ear** forms at the top. The ear is where the wheat **grains** are.

Do you know what straw can be used for?

(answer on page 23)

wheat grains

At **harvest** time, a **combine** cuts down the wheat and removes the grains.

The rest of the plant is left in the field to dry into straw.

10

Farmers sell the grains to flour mills.

At a mill, the grains are crushed to make flour. The flour is sold to bakeries and to supermarkets.

flour

At a bakery, flour is mixed with water, sugar, and yeast to make dough.

The dough is **kneaded**, then baked in an oven. . .

. . .to make bread!

Where do eggs come from?

a) elephants

b) chickens

c) underground

d) humans

(Turn the page to find out.)

11

Where do eggs come from?

Eggs come from hens.
Hens are female chickens.

Hens live on **poultry** farms, in hen houses. They are usually kept in cages. **Free-range** hens live outdoors.

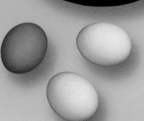

Hens that live on poultry farms eat lots of grain.

grain

Each hen lays an egg almost every day.

The eggs are collected underneath the cages. Rollers gently move the eggs to a packing area, where they are put into trays.

Then the eggs are sent to a **grading station** to be washed and **candled**.

Next, the eggs are sorted by size, and they are put into cartons.

The cartons of eggs are sent to grocery stores and supermarkets.

What other birds' eggs do people eat?

(answer on page 23)

An egg's final stop is on your breakfast table!

Which of these foods come from cows?

a) cheese

b) ice cream

c) yogurt

d) butter

(Turn the page to find out.)

Which foods come from cows?

Milk comes from cows.

Cheese, ice cream, yogurt, and butter are all made from milk.

Cows live on farms. They eat green grass and special feed.

A cow makes milk when it has a calf. The calf drinks some of the milk. A farmer collects the rest.

udder

14

A milking machine is attached to the cow's **udder**. Milk comes out of the udder and is pumped into a storage tank.

Big trucks take the milk to a **dairy**.

Some milk goes to factories to make cheese, ice cream, yogurt, and butter.

What other animals make milk that people drink?

(answer on page 23)

At the dairy, milk is **pasteurized** to kill germs. Then the milk is poured into cartons and bottles.

You buy the cartons and bottles of milk at a grocery store.

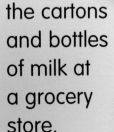

Where does orange juice come from?

a) an animal

b) the sea

c) a fruit tree

d) underground

(Turn the page to find out.)

Where does orange juice come from?

Orange juice comes from oranges.

Oranges are fruits that grow on trees in orange **groves**.

Orange trees grow in places that are warm and sunny almost all year round. These places include Brazil, Spain, and Florida in the United States.

When oranges are ripe, they are picked by hand and are put into big bins.

A truck takes the oranges to a factory.

The oranges are put on a **conveyor belt**. First, they are washed. Then, they are sent through **extractors**, which squeeze out the juice.

What other fruits are made into juice?

(answer on page 23)

The juice is pasteurized to kill germs.

Then it is put into cartons, bottles, and cans. Drink up!

What kind of a plant is rice?

a) a kind of grass

b) a kind of fruit tree

c) a kind of cactus

d) a kind of pond plant

(Turn the page to find out.)

What kind of a plant is rice?

Rice is a kind of grass. It is a **cereal** plant.

Rice is grown in a field called a paddy. A paddy is flooded with water that is 2 to 4 inches (5 to 10 centimeters) deep.

Rice plants need to stay covered with water while they grow.

When the rice is ready to harvest, it is picked either by hand or by a combine.

Can you name another cereal plant?

(answer on page 23)

Then the rice is dried and is taken to a mill.

At the mill, the rice **kernels** are separated from the **husks**.

Broken rice kernels are crushed to make rice flour. The husks are used to make animal feed.

Whole rice kernels are sent to factories. The rice is packed into bags and boxes — ready for you to cook!

What is chocolate made from?

a) bugs

b) birds

c) beans

d) flowers

(Turn the page to find out.)

What is chocolate made from?

Chocolate is made from cocoa beans. Cocoa beans are seeds from the fruit of the cacao tree.

cacao tree fruit

Cacao trees grow in warm, **tropical** countries, such as Brazil and Indonesia.

After the fruit is picked, the beans are left in the Sun to dry.

The dried cocoa beans are sent to a chocolate maker to be **roasted** and crushed into a liquid.

cocoa beans

Some of the liquid is dried to make cocoa powder.

For chocolate bars, the liquid is blended with sugar and milk to make a paste.

The chocolate paste is heated, then slowly cooled. While it cools, nuts or fruits may be added.

What is cocoa powder used for?

(answer on page 23)

chocolate paste

The paste is poured into **molds**.

As it cools, it hardens. Then the chocolate is ready for wrapping.

Now you can unwrap it and eat it!

GLOSSARY

bins: boxlike containers that are usually made of metal or sturdy plastic and are used for storage.

candled: held up to a bright light so the insides can be seen to make sure the egg is not cracked or damaged.

cereal: a type of grass plant that produces grains that can be used for food.

combine: a machine that cuts a grain or cereal plant and removes the seeds.

conveyor belt: a machine with a long, wide, motorized belt that moves objects from one work area of a factory to the next without stopping.

dairy: a place where milk from farms is pasteurized and prepared to be sold.

ear: the part of a cereal plant that holds the grains.

extractors: machines that remove something from an object or separate the parts of an object.

free-range: able to move around, to look for food, in an area that is not enclosed, instead of being kept in a pen or a cage.

grading station: a place where eggs are inspected and measured before they are sorted and packaged.

grains: the seeds of a cereal plant, such as wheat or rice.

groves: places where many fruit trees or nut trees have been planted together, usually in rows.

harvest: (v) to pick or gather crops or fruits that are ripe and ready to eat.

husks: the outer shells of seeds, which are usually peeled, pulled, or broken off and thrown away.

kernels: the soft parts of seeds found inside the husks.

kneaded: folded, pressed, poked, and stretched with the hands and the fingers.

molds: shaped containers that hold runny substances in place until they harden.

pasteurized: heated to a very hot temperature to kill germs.

poultry: birds, such as ducks, chickens, and turkeys, that are raised on farms for their eggs or meat.

produce: (n) fresh plant foods, especially vegetables and fruits, that are grown on farms and in gardens.

ripe: fully grown and ready to be picked.

roasted: cooked in an oven, in dry heat, becoming drier and darker in color.

shoots: small, undeveloped stems and leaves growing out of seeds that have sprouted.

sprout: (v) to produce new growth. (n) the beginning growth of a plant.

tropical: having weather that is hot and damp almost all the time.

udder: the baglike, milk-producing gland that hangs from the abdomen of a cow.

vat: a very large tub, barrel, or tank for holding liquid or semi-liquid substances during various stages of preparation, especially when the process of preparing the substance requires heating or cooking.

Could you answer all the questions? Here are the answers.

page 7: Potato chips are made from potatoes.

page 8: Most people think that tomatoes are vegetables, but they are fruits! Fruits have seeds inside them. Most vegetables do not have seeds inside them.

page 10: Straw can be used as food and bedding material for animals. It can also be used to weave baskets.

page 13: Some people eat ducks' eggs, and some people eat quails' eggs.

page 15: Some people drink goats' milk and sheeps' milk.

page 17: Juice can be made from almost any fruit, but some of the most popular fruit juices are orange, apple, grapefruit, grape, and pineapple.

page 19: Wheat, oats, barley, and rye are all cereal plants.

page 21: Cocoa powder is used to make hot chocolate drinks as well as chocolate cake.

INDEX

B

bakeries 5, 11
bread 9, 10, 11
butter 13, 14, 15

C

cacao 20
cereal plants 18, 19
cheese 13, 14, 15

chickens 12
chocolate 19, 20, 21
cocoa 20, 21
cows 13, 14, 15

D

dairies 15

E

eggs 11, 12, 13

F

farms 5, 6, 8, 12, 14
flour 11, 19
french fries 6, 7, 9
fruits 8, 15, 16, 17,
  20, 21

G

gardens 6, 8
grains 10, 11, 12

H

hamburgers 9
hens 12

I

ice cream 13, 14, 15

K

ketchup 7, 8, 9

M

milk 14, 15

O

orange juice 15, 16, 17
oranges 16, 17

P

potatoes 6, 7, 9

R

rice 17, 18, 19

S

straw 10

T

tomatoes 7, 8, 9

V

vegetables 8

W

wheat 9, 10

Y

yogurt 13, 14, 15